ANDREW M. CUOMO
GOVERNOR

 NEW YORK
STATE OF
OPPORTUNITY

Departme
of State

D0724679

REVISED: March 31, 2020

GUIDANCE TO NOTARIES CONCERNING EXECUTIVE ORDER 202.7

EXECUTIVE ORDER

In response to the COVID-19 (Novel Coronavirus) public health emergency, on March 19, 2020 Governor Cuomo signed Executive Order 202.7, which authorizes notary publics to officiate documents remotely. Specific procedures must be followed to remotely notarize a document. To help the public and notaries public understand the Executive Order, the Department has prepared this guidance.

WHAT IS ALLOWED?

The Executive Order allows a notary public to witness a document being signed, using audio-video technology, and to then notarize the document.

WHAT IS REQUIRED?

To remotely notarize a document, the following conditions must be satisfied:
1. The person seeking the Notary's services, if not personally known to the Notary, must present a valid photo ID to the Notary during the video conference, not merely transmit it prior to or after;
2. The video conference must allow for direct interaction between the person and the Notary (e.g. no pre-recorded videos of the person signing);
3. The person must affirmatively represent that he or she is physically situated in the State of New York;
4. The person must transmit by fax or electronic means a legible copy of the signed document directly to the Notary on the same date it was signed;
5. The Notary may notarize the transmitted copy of the document and transmit the same back to the person; and
6. The Notary may repeat the notarization of the original signed document as of the date of execution provided the Notary receives such original signed document together with the electronically notarized copy within thirty days after the date of execution.

ADDITIONAL CONSIDERATIONS

➢ Notary publics using audio-video technology must continue to follow existing requirements for notarizations that were unaltered by the Executive Order. This includes, but is not limited to, placing the notary's expiration date and county where the notary is commissioned upon the document.

HALF HOLLOW HILLS
COMMUNITY LIBRARY
55 Vanderbilt Parkway
Dix Hills, NY 11746

- If the notary and signatory are in different counties, the notary should indicate on the document the county where each person is located.

- An electronically transmitted document sent to the notary can be sent in any electronic format (e.g., PDF, JPEG, TIFF), provided it is a legible copy.

- The notary must print and sign the document, in ink, and may not use an electronic signature to officiate the document.

- The signatory may use an electronic signature, provided the document can be signed electronically under the Electronic Signatures and Records Act (Article 3 of the State Technology Law). If the signer uses an electronic signature, the notary must witness the electronic signature being applied to the document, as required under Executive Order 202.7.

- The Executive Order does not authorize other officials to administer oaths or to take acknowledgments, and only applies to notary publics commissioned by the Secretary of State's office.

- Following remote notarization, if the notary receives the original document within 30 days, the notary may notarize the document again (i.e., physically affixing a notary stamp and hand signing the document) using the original remote notary date.

- Additionally, when performing remote notarization pursuant to this Executive Order, the Department recommends the following best practices. (However, not following these two recommendations *will not* invalidate the act or be cause for discipline):

  - Keep a notary log of each remote notarization;

  - Indicate on the document that the notarization was made pursuant to Executive Order 202.7.

If you have questions regarding notary practices, please email them to the Department at: licensing@dos.ny.gov or contact (518) 474-4429. Call Center Representatives are available from 8:30am to 4:30pm Monday through Friday except on Legal Holidays.

ALBANY OFFICE:
One Commerce Plaza, 99 Washington Avenue, P.O. Box 22001, Albany, NY 12201-2001
Customer Service: (518) 474-4429 • Website: www.dos.ny.gov • E-Mail: licensing@dos.ny.gov

REGIONAL OFFICES:
• BINGHAMTON • BUFFALO • HAUPPAUGE • NEW YORK CITY • SYRACUSE • UTICA

Notaries public are commissioned by the Secretary of State. An applicant for a notary public commission must submit to the Division of Licensing Services an original application and $60 fee. The application includes an oath of office, which must be sworn and notarized. In addition to the application form and fee, the applicant must submit a "pass slip" showing that s/he has taken and passed the notary public examination. Examinations are regularly scheduled throughout the state. An individual admitted to practice in NYS as an attorney, may be appointed a notary public without an examination. The term of commission is 4 years.

Notaries public are commissioned in their counties of residence. After receiving and approving an applicant for a notary public commission, the Secretary of State forwards the commission, the original oath of office and the signature of the notary public to the appropriate county clerk. The county clerk maintains a record of the commission and signature. The public may then access this record and verify the "official" signature of the notary at the county clerk's office.

Upon request, county clerks will authenticate the signature of the notary on a document and will attest to the notary's authority to sign. This is normally obtained when the documents will be used outside the State. Notaries who expect to sign documents regularly in counties other than that of their residence may elect to file a certificate of official character with other New York State county clerks.

Out-of-State Residents. Attorneys, residing out of State, who are admitted to practice in the State and who maintain a law office within the State are deemed to be residents of the county where the office is maintained. Nonresidents other than attorneys who have offices or places of business in New York State may also become notaries. The oath of office and signature of the notary must be filed in the office of the county clerk of the county in which the office or place of business is located.

NOTARY PUBLIC LICENSE LAW
Table of Contents

REAL PROPERTY LAW

SPECIAL NOTE   25

RESTRICTIONS AND VIOLATIONS JUDICIARY LAW

PUBLIC OFFICERS LAW

EXECUTIVE LAW

PENAL LAW

Use of the office of notary in other than the specific, step-by-step procedure required is viewed as a serious offense by the Secretary of State. The practice of taking acknowledgments and affidavits over the telephone, or otherwise, without the actual, personal appearance of the individual making the acknowledgment or affidavit before the officiating notary, is illegal.

The attention of all notaries public is called to the following judicial declarations concerning such misconduct:

> "The court again wishes to express its condemnation of the acts of notaries taking acknowledgments or affidavits without the presence of the party whose acknowledgment is taken for the affiant, and that it will treat serious professional misconduct the act of any notary thus violating his official duty." (*Matter of Napolis*, 169 App. Div. 469, 472.)

> "Upon the faith of these acknowledgments rests the title of real property, and the only security to such titles is the fidelity with which notaries and commissioners of deeds perform their duty in requiring the appearance of parties to such instruments before them and always refusing to execute a certificate unless the parties are actually known to them or the identity of the parties executing the instruments is satisfactorily proved." (*Matter of Gottheim*, 153 App. Div. 779, 782.)

Equally unacceptable to the Secretary of State is slipshod administration of oaths. **The simplest form in which an oath may be lawfully administered is:**

> **"Do you solemnly swear that the contents of this affidavit subscribed by you is correct and true?"** (Bookman v. City of New York, 200 N.Y. 53, 56.)

Alternatively, the following affirmation may be used for persons who conscientiously decline taking an oath. This affirmation is legally equivalent to an oath and is just as binding:

> **"Do you solemnly, sincerely and truly declare and affirm that the statements made by you are true and correct?"**

Whatever the form adopted, it must be in the presence of an officer authorized to administer it, and it must be an unequivocal and present act by which the affiant consciously takes upon himself the obligation of an oath. (Idem, citing People ex rel. Kenyon v. Sutherland, 81 N.Y. 1; O'Reilly v. People, 86 N.Y. 154, 158, 161.)

Unless a lawyer, the notary public may not engage directly or indirectly in the practice of law. Listed below are some of the activities involving the practice of law which are prohibited, and which subject the notary public to removal from office by the Secretary of State, and possible imprisonment, fine or both. A notary:

1.) **May not give advice on the law.** The notary may not draw any kind of legal papers, such as wills, deeds, bills of sale, mortgages, chattel mortgages, contracts, leases, offers, options, incorporation papers, releases, mechanics liens, power of attorney, complaints and all legal pleadings, papers in summary proceedings to evict a tenant, or in bankruptcy, affidavits, or any papers which our courts have said are legal documents or papers.

2.) **May not ask for and get legal business** to send to a lawyer or lawyers with whom he has any business connection or from whom he receives any money or other consideration for sending the business.

3.) **May not divide or agree to divide** his fees with a lawyer, or accept any part of a lawyer's fee on any legal business.

4.) **May not advertise in, or circulate** in any manner, any paper or advertisement, or say to anyone that he has any powers or rights not given to the notary by the laws under which the notary was appointed.

A notary public is cautioned not to execute an acknowledgment of the execution of a will. Such acknowledgment cannot be deemed equivalent to an attestation clause accompanying a will.

(See definition of Attestation Clause)

APPOINTMENT AND QUALIFICATIONS

§130. Appointment of notaries public

1. The Secretary of State may appoint and commission as many notaries public for the State of New York as in his or her judgment may be deemed best, whose jurisdiction shall be co-extensive with the boundaries of the state. The appointment of a notary public shall be for a term of 4 years. An application for an appointment as notary public shall be in form and set forth such matters as the Secretary of State shall prescribe. Every person appointed as notary public must, at the time of his or her appointment, be a citizen of the United States and either a resident of the State of New York or have an office or place of business in New York State. A notary public who is a resident of the State and who moves out of the state but still maintains a place of business or an office in New York State does not vacate his or her office as a notary public. A notary public who is a nonresident and who ceases to have an office or place of business in this state, vacates his or her office as a notary public. A notary public who is a resident of New York State and moves out of the state and who does not retain an office or place of business in this State shall vacate his or her office as a notary public. A non-resident who accepts the office of notary public in this State

7

thereby appoints the Secretary of State as the person upon whom process can be served on his or her behalf. Before issuing to any applicant a commission as notary public, unless he or she be an attorney and counselor at law duly admitted to practice in this state or a court clerk of the Unified Court System who has been appointed to such position after taking a Civil Service promotional examination in the court clerk series of titles, the Secretary of State shall satisfy himself or herself that the applicant is of good moral character, has the equivalent of a common school education and is familiar with the duties and responsibilities of a notary public; provided, however, that where a notary public applies, before the expiration of his or her term, for reappointment with the county clerk or where a person whose term as notary public shall have expired applies within 6 months thereafter for reappointment as a notary public with the county clerk, such qualifying requirements may be waived by the Secretary of State, and further, where an application for reappointment is filed with the county clerk after the expiration of the aforementioned renewal period by a person who failed or was unable to re-apply by reason of his or her induction or enlistment in the armed forces of the United States, such qualifying requirements may also be waived by the Secretary of State, provided such application for reappointment is made within a period of 1 year after the military discharge of the applicant under conditions other than dishonorable. In any case, the appointment or reappointment of any applicant is in the discretion of the Secretary of State. The Secretary of State may suspend or remove from office, for misconduct, any notary public appointed by him or her but no such removal shall be made unless the person who is sought to be removed shall have been served with a copy of the charges against him or her and have an opportunity of being heard. No person shall be appointed as a notary public under this article who has been convicted, in this State or any other state or territory, of a crime, unless the secretary makes a finding in conformance with all applicable statutory requirements, including those contained in article twenty-three-A of the correction law, that such convictions do not constitute a bar to appointment.

2. A person regularly admitted to practice as an attorney and counselor in the courts of record of this state, whose office for the practice of law is within the State, may be appointed a notary public and retain his office as such notary public although he resides in or removes to an adjoining state. For the purpose of this and the following sections of this article such person shall be deemed a resident of the county where he maintains such office.

§131. Procedure of appointment; fees and commissions

1. Applicants for a notary public commission shall submit to the Secretary of State with their application the oath of office, duly executed before any person authorized to administer an oath, together with their signature.

8

2. Upon being satisfied of the competency and good character of applicants for appointment as notaries public, the Secretary of State shall issue a commission to such persons; and the official signature of the applicants and the oath of office filed with such applications shall take effect.

3. The Secretary of State shall receive a non-refundable application fee of $60 from applicants for appointment, which fee shall be submitted together with the application. No further fee shall be paid for the issuance of the commission.

4. A notary public identification card indicating the appointee's name, address, county and commission term shall be transmitted to the appointee.

5. The commission, duly dated, and a certified copy or the original of the oath of office and the official signature, and $20 apportioned from the application fee shall be transmitted by the Secretary of State to the county clerk in which the appointee resides by the 10th day of the following month.

6. The county clerk shall make a proper index of commissions and official signatures transmitted to that office by the Secretary of State pursuant to the provisions of this section.

7. Applicants for reappointment of a notary public commission shall submit to the county clerk with their application the oath of office, duly executed before any person authorized to administer an oath, together with their signature.

8. Upon being satisfied of the completeness of the application for reappointment, the county clerk shall issue a commission to such persons; and the official signature of the applicants and the oath of office filed with such applications shall take effect.

9. The county clerk shall receive a non-refundable application fee of $60 from each applicant for reappointment, which fee shall be submitted together with the application. No further fee shall be paid for the issuance of the commission.

10. The commission, duly dated, and a certified or original copy of the application, and $40 apportioned from the application fee plus interest as may be required by statute shall be transmitted by the county clerk to the Secretary of State by the 10th day of the following month.

11. The Secretary of State shall make a proper record of commissions transmitted to that office by the county clerk pursuant to the provisions of this section.

12. Except for changes made in an application for reappointment, the Secretary of State shall receive a non-refundable fee of $10 for changing the name or address of a notary public.

13. The Secretary of State may issue a duplicate identification card to a notary public for one lost, destroyed or damaged upon application therefor on a form prescribed by the Secretary of State and upon payment of a non-refundable fee of $10. Each such duplicate identification card shall have the word "duplicate"

stamped across the face thereof, and shall bear the same number as the one it replaces.

§132. Certificates of official character of notaries public

The Secretary of State or the county clerk of the county in which the commission of a notary public is filed may certify to the official character of such notary public and any notary public may file his autograph signature and a certificate of official character in the office of any county clerk of any county in the State and in any register's office in any county having a register and thereafter such county clerk may certify as to the official character of such notary public. The Secretary of State shall collect for each certificate of official character issued by him the sum of one dollar. The county clerk and register of any county with whom a certificate of official character has been filed shall collect for filing the same the sum of one dollar. For each certificate of official character issued, with seal attached, by any county clerk, the sum of one dollar shall be collected by him.

§133. Certification of notarial signatures

The county clerk of a county in whose office any notary public has qualified or has filed his autograph signature and a certificate of his official character, shall, when so requested and upon payment of a fee of $3 affix to any certificate of proof or acknowledgment or oath signed by such notary anywhere in the State of New York, a certificate under his hand and seal, stating that a commission or a certificate of his official character with his autograph signature has been filed in his office, and that he was at the time of taking such proof or acknowledgment or oath duly authorized to take the same; that he is well acquainted with the handwriting of such notary public or has compared the signature on the certificate of proof or acknowledgment or oath with the autograph signature deposited in his office by such notary public and believes that the signature is genuine. An instrument with such certificate of authentication of the county clerk affixed thereto shall be entitled to be read in evidence or to be recorded in any of the counties of this State in respect to which a certificate of a county clerk may be necessary for either purpose.

§140. Executive Law

14. No person who has been removed from office as a commissioner of deeds for the City of New York, as hereinbefore provided, shall thereafter be eligible again to be appointed as such commissioner nor, shall he be eligible thereafter to appoint to the office of notary public.

15. Any person who has been removed from office as aforesaid, who shall, after

knowledge of such removal, sign or execute any instrument as a commissioner of deeds or notary public shall be deemed guilty of a misdemeanor.

§3-200 and 3-400. Election Law

A commissioner of elections or inspector of elections is eligible for the office of notary public.

§3. Public Officers Law

No person is eligible for the office of notary public who has been convicted of a violation of the selective draft act of the U.S. enacted May 18, 1917, or the acts amendatory or supplemental thereto, or of the federal selective training and service act of 1940 or the acts amendatory thereof or supplemental thereto.

§534. County Law

Each county clerk shall designate from among the members of his or her staff at least one notary public to be available to notarize documents for the public in each county clerk's office during normal business hours free of charge. Each individual appointed by the county clerk to be a notary public pursuant to this section shall be exempt from the examination fee and application fee required by §131 of the Executive Law.

Miscellaneous

Member of legislature

"If a member of the legislature be *** appointed to any office, civil *** under the government *** the State of New York *** his or her acceptance thereof shall vacate his or her seat in the legislature, providing, however, that a member of the legislature may be appointed *** to any office in which he or she shall receive no compensation." (§7 of Article III of the Constitution of the State of New York.) A member of the legislature may be appointed a notary public in view of transfer of power of such appointment from the governor and senate to the Secretary of State. (1927, Op. Atty. Gen. 97.)

Sheriffs

*** Sheriffs shall hold no other office. *** (§13(a) of Article XIII of the Constitution of the State of New York.)

Notary public—disqualifications.

Though a person may be eligible to hold the office of notary the person may be disqualified to act in certain cases by reason of having an interest in the case. To state the rule broadly: if the notary is a party to or directly and pecuniarily interested in the transaction, the person is not capable of acting in that case. For example, a notary who is a grantee or mortgagee in a conveyance or mortgage is disqualified to take the acknowledgment of the grantor or mortgagor; likewise a notary who is a trustee in a deed of trust; and, of course, a notary who is the grantor could not take his own acknowledgment. A notary beneficially interested in the conveyance by way of being secured thereby is not competent to take the acknowledgment of the instrument. In New York the courts have held an acknowledgment taken by a person financially or beneficially interested in a party to conveyance or instrument of which it is a part to be a nullity; and that the acknowledgment of an assignment of a mortgage before one of the assignees is a nullity; and that an acknowledgment by one of the incorporators of the other incorporators who signed a certificate was of no legal effect.

POWERS AND DUTIES

§134. Signature and seal of county clerk

The signature and seal of a county clerk, upon a certificate of official character of a notary public or the signature of a county clerk upon a certificate of authentication of the signature and acts of a notary public or commissioner of deeds, may be a facsimile, printed, stamped, photographed or engraved thereon.

13

§135. Powers and duties; in general; of notaries public who are at attorneys at law

Every notary public duly qualified is hereby authorized and empowered within and throughout the State to administer oaths and affirmations, to take affidavits and depositions, to receive and certify acknowledgments or proof of deeds, mortgages and powers of attorney and other instruments in writing; to demand acceptance or payment of foreign and inland bills of exchange, promissory notes and obligations in writing, and to protest the same for non-acceptance or non-payment, as the case may require, and, for use in another jurisdiction, to exercise such other powers and duties as by the laws of nations and according to commercial usage, or by the laws of any other government or country may be exercised and performed by notaries public, provided that when exercising such powers he shall set forth the name of such other jurisdiction.

A notary public who is an attorney at law regularly admitted to practice in this State may, in his discretion, administer an oath or affirmation to or take the affidavit or acknowledgment of his client in respect of any matter, claim, action or proceeding.

For any misconduct by a notary public in the performance of any of his powers such notary public shall be liable to the parties injured for all damages sustained by them. A notary public shall not, directly or indirectly, demand or receive for the protest for the non-payment of any note, or for the non-acceptance or non-payment of any bill of exchange, check or draft and giving the requisite notices and certificates of such protest, including his notarial seal, if affixed thereto, any greater fee or reward than 75 cents for such protest, and 10 cents for each notice, not exceeding five, on any bill or note. Every notary public having a seal shall, except as otherwise provided, and when requested, affix his seal to such protest free of expense.

§135-a. Notary public or commissioner of deeds; acting without appointment; fraud in office

1. Any person who holds himself out to the public as being entitled to act as a notary public or commissioner of deeds, or who assumes, uses or advertises the title of notary public or commissioner of deeds, or equivalent terms in any language, in such a manner as to convey the impression that he is a notary public or commissioner of deeds without having first been appointed as notary public or commissioner of deeds, or

2. A notary public or commissioner of deeds, who in the exercise of the powers, or in the performance of the duties of such office shall practice any fraud or

14

deceit, the punishment for which is not otherwise provided for by this act, shall be guilty of a misdemeanor.

§135-b. Advertising by notaries public

1. The provisions of this section shall not apply to attorneys-at-law, admitted to practice in the state of New York.

2. A notary public who advertises his or her services as a notary public in a language other than English shall post with such advertisement a notice in such other language the following statement: "I am not an attorney licensed to practice law and may not give legal advice about immigration or any other legal matter or accept fees for legal advice."

3. A notary public shall not use terms in a foreign language in any advertisement for his or her services as a notary public that mean or imply that the notary public is an attorney licensed to practice in the state of New York or in any jurisdiction of the United States. The secretary shall designate by rule or regulation the terms in a foreign language that shall be deemed to mean or imply that a notary public is licensed to practice law in the state of New York and the use of which shall be prohibited by notary publics who are subject to this section.

4. For purposes of this section, "advertisement" shall mean and include material designed to give notice of or to promote or describe the services offered by a notary public for profit and shall include business cards, brochures, and notices, whether in print or electronic form.

5. Any person who violates any provision of this section or any rule or regulation promulgated by the secretary may be liable for civil penalty of up to one thousand dollars. The secretary of state may suspend a notary public upon a second violation of any of the provisions of this section and may remove from office a notary public upon a third violation of any of the provisions of this section, provided that the notary public shall have been served with a copy of the charges against him or her and been given an opportunity to be heard. The civil penalty provided for by this subdivision shall be recoverable in an action instituted by the attorney general on his or her own initiative or at the request of the secretary.

6. The secretary may promulgate rules and regulations governing the provisions of this section, including the size and type of statements that a notary public is required by this section to post.

§136. Notarial fees.

A notary public shall be entitled to the following fees:

1. For administering an oath or affirmation, and certifying the same when required, except where another fee is specifically prescribed by statute, $2.

2. For taking and certifying the acknowledgment or proof of execution of a written instrument, by one person, $2, and by each additional person, $2, for swearing such witness thereto, $2.

§137. Statement as to authority of notaries public.

In exercising his powers pursuant to this article, a notary public, in addition to the venue of his act and his signature, shall print, typewrite, or stamp beneath his signature in black ink, his name, the words "Notary Public State of New York," the name of the county in which he originally qualified, and the date upon which his commission expires and, in addition, wherever required, a notary public shall also include the name of any county in which his certificate of official character is filed, using the words "Certificate filed .... County." A notary public who is duly licensed as an attorney and counselor at law in this State may in his discretion, substitute the words "Attorney and Counselor at Law" for the words "Notary Public." A notary public who has qualified or who has filed a certificate of official character in the office of the clerk in a county or counties within the City of New York must also affix to each instrument his official number or numbers in black ink, as given to him by the clerk or clerks of such county or counties at the time such notary qualified in such county or counties and, if the instrument is to be recorded in an office of the register of the City of New York in any county within such city and the notary has been given a number or numbers by such register or his predecessors in any county or counties, when his autographed signature and certificate are filed in such office or offices pursuant to this chapter, he shall also affix such number or numbers. No official act of such notary public shall be held invalid on account of the failure to comply with these provisions. If any notary public shall wilfully fail to comply with any of the provisions of this section, he shall be subject to disciplinary action by the secretary of state. In all the courts within this State the certificate of a notary public, over his signature, shall be received as presumptive evidence of the facts contained in such certificate; provided, that any person interested as a party to a suit may contradict, by other evidence, the certificate of a notary public.

§138. Powers of notaries public or other officers who are stock-holders, directors, officers or employees of a corporation.

A notary public, justice of the supreme court, a judge, clerk, deputy clerk, or special deputy clerk of a court, an official examiner of title, or the mayor or recorder of a city, a justice of the peace, surrogate, special surrogate, special county judge, or commissioner of deeds, who is a stockholder, director, officer or employee of a corporation may take the acknowledgment or proof of any party to a written instrument executed to or by such corporation, or administer an oath of any other stockholder, director, officer, employee or agent of such corporation, and such notary public may protest for non- acceptance or non-payment, bills of exchange, drafts, checks, notes and other negotiable instruments owned or held for collection by such corporation; but none of the officers above named shall take the acknowledgment or proof of a written instrument by or to a corporation of which he is a stockholder, director, officer or employee, if such officer taking such acknowledgment or proof to be a party executing such instrument, either individually or as representative of such corporation, nor shall a notary public protest any negotiable instruments owned or held for collection by such corporation, if such notary public be individually a party to such instrument, or have a financial interest in the subject of same. All such acknowledgments or proofs of deeds, mortgages or other written instruments, relating to real property heretofore taken before any of the officers aforesaid are confirmed. This act shall not affect any action or legal proceeding now pending.

§142-a. Validity of acts of notaries public and commissioners of deeds notwithstanding certain defects.

1. Except as provided in subdivision three of this section, the official certificates and other acts heretofore or hereafter made or performed of notaries public and commissioners of deeds heretofore or hereafter and prior to the time of their acts appointed or commissioned as such shall not be deemed invalid, impaired or in any manner defective, so far as they may be affected, impaired or questioned by reason of defects described in subdivision two of this section.

2. This section shall apply to the following defects:

    (a) ineligibility of the notary public or commissioner of deeds to be appointed or commissioned as such;

    (b) misnomer or misspelling of name or other error made in his appointment or commission;

    (c) omission of the notary public or commissioner of deeds to take or file his official oath or otherwise qualify;

(d) expiration of his term, commission or appointment;

(e) vacating of his office by change of his residence, by acceptance of another public office, or by other action on his part;

(f) the fact that the action was taken outside the jurisdiction where the notary public or commissioner of deeds was authorized to act.

3. No person shall be entitled to assert the effect of this section to overcome a defect described in subdivision two if he knew of the defect or if the defect was apparent on the face of the certificate of the notary public or commissioner of deeds; provided however, that this subdivision shall not apply after the expiration of six months from the date of the act of the notary public or commissioner of deeds.

4. After the expiration of six months from the date of the official certificate or other act of the commissioner of deeds, subdivision one of this section shall be applicable to a defect consisting in omission of the certificate of a commissioner of deeds to state the date on which and the place in which an act was done, or consisting of an error in such statement.

5. This section does not relieve any notary public or commissioner of deeds from criminal liability imposed by reason of his act, or enlarge the actual authority of any such officer, nor limit any other statute or rule of law by reason of which the act of a notary public or commissioner of deeds, or the record thereof, is valid or is deemed valid in any case.

REAL PROPERTY LAW
§290. Definitions; effect of article

The term "conveyance" includes every written instrument, by which any estate or interest in real property is created, transferred, mortgaged or assigned, or by which the title to any real property may be affected, including an instrument in execution of power, although the power be one of revocation only, and an instrument postponing or subordinating a mortgage lien; except a will, a lease for a term not exceeding three years, an executory contract for the sale or purchase of lands, and an instrument containing a power to convey real property as the agent or attorney for the owner of such property.

§298. Acknowledgments and proofs within the state

The acknowledgment or proof, within this state, of a conveyance of real property situate in this State may be made:

1. At any place within the state, before
   a) a justice of the supreme court;
   b) an official examiner of title;
   c) an official referee; or
   d) a notary public.

2. Within the district wherein such officer is authorized to perform official duties, before
   (a) a judge or clerk of any court of record;
   (b) a commissioner of deeds outside of the City of New York, or a commissioner of deeds of the City of New York within the five counties comprising the City of New York;
   (c) the mayor or recorder of a city;
   (d) a surrogate, special surrogate, or special county judge; or
   (e) the county clerk or other recording officer of a county.

3. Before a justice of the peace, town councilman, village police justice or a judge of any court of inferior local jurisdiction, anywhere within the county containing the town, village or city in which he is authorized to perform official duties.

§302. Acknowledgments and proofs by married women

The acknowledgment or proof of a conveyance of real property, within the state, or of any other written instrument, may be made by a married woman the same as if unmarried.

§303. Requisites of acknowledgments

An acknowledgment must not be taken by any officer unless he knows or has satisfactory evidence, that the person making it is the person described in and who executed such instrument.

§304. Proof by subscribing witness

When the execution of a conveyance is proved by a subscribing witness, such witness must state his own place of residence, and if his place of residence is in a city, the street and street number, if any thereof, and that he knew the person described in and who executed the conveyance. The proof must not be taken unless the officer is personally acquainted with such witness, or has satisfactory evidence that he is the same person, who was a subscribing witness to the conveyance.

§306. Certificate of acknowledgment or proof

A person taking the acknowledgment or proof of a conveyance must endorse thereupon or attach thereto, a certificate, signed by himself, stating all the matters required to be done, known, or proved on the taking of such acknowledgment or proof; together with the name and substance of the testimony of each witness examined before him, and if a subscribing witness, his place of residence.

§309-a. Uniform forms of certificates of acknowledgment or proof within this state.

1. The certificate of an acknowledgment, within this State, or a conveyance or other instrument in respect to real property situate in this State, by a person, must conform substantially with the following form, the blanks being properly filled:

State of New York)

) ss.:

County of _____)

On the _____ day of _____ in the year _____ before me, the undersigned, personally appeared _____, personally known to me or proved to me on the basis of satisfactory evidence to be the individual(s) whose name(s) is (are) subscribed to the within instrument and acknowledged to me that he/she/they executed the same in his/her/their capacity(ies), and that by his/her/their signature(s) on the instrument, the individual(s), or the person upon behalf of which the individual(s) acted, executed the instrument.

(Signature and office of individual taking acknowledgment.)

2. The certificate for a proof of execution by a subscribing witness, within this state, of a conveyance or other instrument made by any person in respect to real property situate in this state, must conform substantially with the following form, the blanks being properly filled:

State of New York)

) ss.:

County of _____)

On the _____ day of _____ in the year _____ before me, the undersigned, personally appeared _____ , the subscribing witness to the foregoing instrument, with whom I am personally acquainted, who, being by me duly sworn, did depose and say that he/she/they reside(s) in _____ (*if the place of residence is in a city, include the street and street number, if any, thereof*); that he/she/they know(s) _____ to be the individual described in and who executed the foregoing instrument; that said subscribing witness was present and saw said _____ execute the same; and that said witness at the same time subscribed his/her/their name(s) as a witness thereto.

(*Signature and office of individual taking proof.*)

3. A certificate of an acknowledgment or proof taken under §300 of this article shall include the additional information required by that section.

4. For the purposes of this section, the term "person" means any corporation, joint stock company, estate, general partnership (including any registered limited liability partnership or foreign limited liability partnership), limited liability company (including a professional service limited liability company), foreign limited liability company (including a foreign professional service limited liability company), joint venture, limited partnership, natural person, attorney in fact, real estate investment trust, business trust or other trust, custodian, nominee or any other individual or entity in its own or any representative capacity.

§ 309-b. Uniform forms of certificates of acknowledgment or proof without this state

1. The certificate of an acknowledgment, without this State, of a conveyance or other instrument with respect to real property situate in this State, by a person, may conform substantially with the following form, the blanks being properly filled:

State, District of Columbia,)

Territory, Possession, or) ss.:

Foreign Country)

On the _____ day of _____ in the year _____ before me, the undersigned, personally appeared _____, personally known to me or proved to me on the basis of satisfactory evidence to be the individual(s) whose name(s) is (are) subscribed to the within instrument and acknowledged to me that he/she/they executed the same in his/her/their capacity(ies), and that by his/her/their signature(s) on the instrument, the individual(s), or the person upon behalf of which the individual(s) acted, executed the instrument.

(*Signature and office of individual taking acknowledgment.*)

2. The certificate for a proof of execution by a subscribing witness, without this State, of a conveyance or other instrument made by any person in respect to real property situate in this State, may conform substantially with the following form, the blanks being properly filled:

State, District of Columbia,)

Territory, Possession, or) ss.:

Foreign Country)

On the _____ day of _____ in the year _____ before me, the undersigned, personally appeared _____, the subscribing witness to the foregoing instrument, with whom I am personally acquainted, who, being by me duly sworn, did depose and say that he/she resides in _____(if the place of residence is in a city, include the street and street number, if any, thereof); that he/she knows _____ to be the individual described in and who executed the foregoing instrument; that said subscribing witness was present and saw said _____ execute the same; and that said witness at the same time subscribed his/her name as a witness thereto.

(*Signature and office of individual taking proof.*)

3. No provision of this section shall be construed to:
   (a) modify the choice of laws afforded by §§299-a and 301-a of this article pursuant to which an acknowledgment or proof may be taken;
   (b) modify any requirement of §307 of this article;
   (c) modify any requirement for a seal imposed by subdivision one of §308 of this article;
   (d) modify any requirement concerning a certificate of authentication imposed by §308, 311, 312, 314, or 318 of this article; or
   (e) modify any requirement imposed by any provision of this article when the certificate of acknowledgment or proof purports to be taken in the manner prescribed by the laws of another state, the District of Columbia, territory, possession, or foreign country.

4. A certificate of an acknowledgment or proof taken under §300 of this article shall include the additional information required by that section.

5. For the purposes of this section, the term "person" means a person as defined

in subdivision 4 of §309-a of this article.

6. The inclusion within the body (other than the jurat) of a certificate of acknowledgment or proof made under this section or the city or other political subdivision and the state or country or other place the acknowledgment was taken shall be deemed. A non-substantial variance from the form of a certificate authorized by this section.

§330. Officers guilty of malfeasance liable for damages

An officer authorized to take the acknowledgment or proof of a conveyance or other instrument, or to certify such proof or acknowledgment, or to record the same, who is guilty of malfeasance or fraudulent practice in the execution of any duty prescribed by law in relation thereto, is liable in damages to the person injured.

§333. When conveyances of real property not to be recorded

. . .

2. A recording officer shall not record or accept for record any conveyance of real property, unless said conveyance in its entirety and the certificate of acknowledgment or proof and the authentication thereof, other than proper names therein which may be in another language provided they are written in English letters or characters, shall be in the English language, or unless such conveyance, certificate of acknowledgment or proof, and the authentication thereof be accompanied by and have attached thereto a translation in the English language duly executed and acknowledged by the person or persons making such conveyance and proved and authenticated, if need be, in the manner required of conveyances for recording in this state, or, unless such conveyance, certificate of acknowledgment or proof, and the authentication thereof be accompanied by and have attached thereto a translation in the English language made by a person duly designated for such purpose by the county judge of the county where it is desired to record such conveyance or a justice of the supreme court and be duly signed, acknowledged and certified under oath or upon affirmation by such person before such judge, to be a true and accurate translation and contain a certification of the designation of such person by such judge.

SPECIAL NOTE

By reason of changes in certain provisions of the Real Property Law, any and all limitations on the authority of a notary public to act as such in any part of the State have been removed; a notary public may now, in addition to administer-

ing oaths or taking affidavits anywhere in the State, take acknowledgments and proofs of conveyances anywhere in the State. The need for a certificate of authentication of a county clerk as a prerequisite to recording or use in evidence in this State of the instrument acknowledged or proved has been abolished. The certificate of authentication may possibly be required where the instrument is to be recorded or used in evidence outside the jurisdiction of the State.

Effective September 23, 2012, recording officers (County Clerks) may receive and record digitized paper documents and electronic records affecting real property, including real property transfer documents such as deeds, mortgages, notes and accompanying documents. The Office of Information Technology Services (ITS) has promulgated rules and regulations to support the implementation of electronic recording by local recording officers.

§335. Banking Law

If the rental fee of any safe deposit box is not paid, or after the termination of the lease for such box, and at least 30 days after giving proper notice to the lessee, the lessor (bank) may, in the presence of a notary public, open the safe deposit box, remove and inventory the contents. The notary public shall then file with the lessor a certificate under seal which states the date of the opening of the safe deposit box, the name of the lessee, and a list of the contents. Within 10 days of the opening of the safe deposit box, a copy of this certificate must be mailed to the lessee at his last known postal address.

Rule 3113. Civil Practice Law and Rules

This rule authorizes a deposition to be taken before a notary public in a civil proceeding.

§11. Domestic Relations Law

A notary public has no authority to solemnize marriages; nor may a notary public take the acknowledgment of parties and witnesses to a written contract of marriage.

§10. Public Officers Law

Official oaths, permits the oath of a public officer to be administered by a notary public.

RESTRICTIONS AND VIOLATIONS

INDEX

JUDICIARY LAW
§484. None but attorneys to practice in the state

No natural person shall ask or receive, directly or indirectly, compensation for appearing for a person other than himself as attorney in any court or before any magistrate, or for preparing deeds, mortgages, assignments, discharges, leases or any other instruments affecting real estate, wills, codicils, or any other instrument affecting the disposition of property after death, or decedents' estates, or pleadings of any kind in any action brought before any court of record in this state, or make it a business to practice for another as an attorney in any court or before any magistrate unless he has been regularly admitted to practice, as an attorney or counselor, in the courts of record in the state; but nothing in this section shall apply

(1) to officers of societies for the prevention of cruelty, duly appointed, when exercising the special powers conferred upon such corporations under §1403 of the Not-for-Profit Corporation Law; or

(2) to law students who have completed at least 2 semesters of law school

or persons who have graduated from a law school, who have taken the examination for admittance to practice law in the courts of record in the state immediately available after graduation from law school, or the examination immediately available after being notified by the board of law examiners that they failed to pass said exam, and who have not been notified by the board of law examiners that they have failed to pass two such examinations, acting under the supervision of a legal aid organization, when such students and persons are acting under a program approved by the appellate division of the supreme court of the department in which the principal office of such organization is located and specifying the extent to which such students and persons may engage in activities prohibited by this statute; or

(3) to persons who have graduated from a law school approved pursuant to the rules of the court of appeals for the admission of attorneys and counselors-at-law and who have taken the examination for admission to practice as an attorney and counselor-at-law immediately available after graduation from law school or the examination immediately available after being notified by the board of law examiners that they failed to pass said exam, and who have not been notified by the board of law examiners that they have failed to pass two such examinations, when such persons are acting under the supervision of the state or a subdivision thereof or of any officer or agency of the state or a subdivision thereof, pursuant to a program approved by the appellate division of the supreme court of the department within which such activities are taking place and specifying the extent to which they may engage in activities otherwise prohibited by this statute and those powers of the supervising governmental entity or officer in connection with which they may engage in such activities.

§485. Violation of certain preceding sections a misdemeanor

Any person violating the provisions of §§478, 479, 480, 481, 482, 483 or 484, shall be guilty of a misdemeanor.

§750. Power of courts to punish for criminal contempts

.   .   .

(B) [T]he supreme court has power under this section to punish for a criminal contempt any person who unlawfully practices or assumes to practice law; and a proceeding under this subdivision may be instituted on the court's own motion or on the motion of any officer charged with the duty of investigating or prosecuting unlawful practice of law, or by any bar association incorporated under the laws of this State.

Illegal practice of law by notary public

To make it a business to practice as an attorney at law, not being a lawyer, is a crime. "Counsel and advice, the drawing of agreements, the organization of corporations and preparing papers connected therewith, the drafting of legal documents of all kinds, including wills, are activities which have been long classed as law practice." (*People v. Alfani*, 227 NY 334, 339.)

Wills

The execution of wills under the supervision of a notary public acting in effect as a lawyer, "cannot be too strongly condemned, not only for the reason that it means an invasion of the legal profession, but for the fact that testators thereby run the risk of frustrating their own solemnly declared intentions and rendering worthless maturely considered plans for the disposition of estates whose creation may have been the fruit of lives of industry and self-denial." (*Matter of Flynn*, 142 Misc. 7.)

Notary must not act before taking and filing oath of office. The Public Officers Law (§15) provides that a person who executes any of the functions of a public office without having taken and duly filed the required oath of office, as prescribed by law, is guilty of a misdemeanor. A notary public is a public officer.

§67. Fees of public officers

1. Each public officer upon whom a duty is expressly imposed by law, must execute the same without fee or reward, except where a fee or other compensation therefor is expressly allowed by law.

2. An officer or other person, to whom a fee or other compensation is allowed by law, for any service, shall not charge or receive a greater fee or reward, for that service, than is so allowed.

3. An officer, or other person, shall not demand or receive any fee or

   compensation, allowed to him by law for any service, unless the service was actually rendered by him; except that an officer may demand in advance his fee, where he is, by law, expressly directed or permitted to require payment thereof, before rendering the service.

4. *** An officer or other person, who violates either of the provisions contained in this section, is liable, in addition to the punishment prescribed by law for the criminal offense, to an action in behalf of the person aggrieved, in which the plaintiff is entitled to treble damages.

A notary public subjects himself to criminal prosecution, civil suit and possible removal by asking or receiving more than the statutory allowance, for administering the ordinary oath in connect with an affidavit. (Op. Atty. Gen. (1917) 12 St. Dept. Rep. 507.)

§69. Fee for administering certain official oaths prohibited.

An officer is not entitled to a fee, for administering the oath of office to a member of the legislature, to any military officer, to an inspector of election, clerk of the poll, or to any other public officer or public employee.

EXECUTIVE LAW
Misconduct by a notary and removal from office

A notary public who, in the performance of the duties of such office shall practice any fraud or deceit, is guilty of a misdemeanor (Executive Law, §135-a), and may be removed from office. The notary may be removed from office if the notary made a misstatement of a material fact in his application for appointment; for preparing and taking an oath of an affiant to a statement that the notary knew to be false or fraudulent.

PENAL LAW
§70.00 Sentence of imprisonment for felony.

. . .

2. Maximum term of sentence. The maximum term of an indeterminate sentence shall be at least three years and the term shall be fixed as follows:

. . .

(d) For a class D felony, the term shall be fixed by the court, and shall not exceed 7 years; and

(e) For a class E felony, the term shall be fixed by the court, and shall not exceed 4 years.

. . .

§70.15 Sentences of imprisonment for misdemeanors and violation

1. Class A misdemeanor. A sentence of imprisonment for a class A misdemeanor shall be a definite sentence. When such a sentence is imposed the term shall be fixed by the court, and shall not exceed one year;

. . .

§170.10 Forgery in the second degree.

A person is guilty of forgery in the second degree when, with intent to defraud, deceive or injure another, he falsely makes, completes or alters a written instrument which is or purports to be, or which is calculated to become or to represent if completed:

1. A deed, will, codicil, contract, assignment, commercial instrument, or other

   instrument which does or may evidence, create, transfer, terminate or otherwise affect a legal right, interest, obligation or status; or

2. A public record, or an instrument filed or required or authorized by law to be filed in or with a public office or public servant; or

3. A written instrument officially issued or created by a public office, public

31

servant or governmental instrumentality.

. . .

Forgery in the second degree is a class D felony.

§175.40 Issuing a false certificate

A person is guilty of issuing a false certificate when, being a public servant authorized by law to make or issue official certificates or other official written instruments, and with intent to defraud, deceive or injure another person, he issues such an instrument, or makes the same with intent that it be issued, knowing that it contains a false statement or false information.

Issuing a false certificate is a class E felony.

§195.00 Official misconduct

A public servant is guilty of official misconduct when, with intent to obtain a benefit or to injure or deprive another person of a benefit:

1. He commits an act relating to his office but constituting an unauthorized exercise of his official functions, knowing that such act is unauthorized; or

2. He knowingly refrains from performing a duty which is imposed upon him by law or is clearly inherent in the nature of his office.

Official misconduct is a class A misdemeanor.

Notary must officiate on request.

The Penal Law (§195.00) provides that an officer before whom an oath or affidavit may be taken is bound to administer the same when requested, and a refusal to do so is a misdemeanor. (*People v. Brooks*, 1 Den. 457.)

Perjury

One is guilty of perjury if he has stated or given testimony on a material matter, under oath or by affirmation, as to the truth thereof, when he knew the statement or testimony to be false and willfully made.

RULES AND REGULATIONS
TITLE 19 NYCRR
CHAPTER V, SUBCHAPTER L
PART 182
NOTARIES PUBLIC

§182.1 Advertising

(a) A notary public who is not an attorney licensed to practice law in the State of New York shall not falsely advertise that he or she is an attorney licensed to practice law in the State of New York or in any jurisdiction of the United States by using foreign terms including, but not limited to: abogado, mandataire, procuratore, Адвокат, 律師, and avoca.

(b) A notary public who is not an attorney licensed to practice law in the State of New York and who advertises his or her services as a notary public in a language other than English shall include in the advertisement the following disclaimer: "I am not an attorney licensed to practice law and may not give legal advice about immigration or any other legal matter or accept fees for legal advice." The disclaimer shall be printed clearly and conspicuously and shall be made in the same language as the advertisement. The translated disclaimer, in some but not all languages, is as follows:

(1) Simplified Chinese:
我不是有执照的律师，不能出庭辩护，不能提供有关移民事务或其他法律事务的法律建议，也不能收取法律咨询的费用。

(2) Traditional Chinese:
本人不是持牌執業律師，因此不能出庭辯護，不能向閣下提供移民及其他法律事務方面的法律意見，也不能收取法律諮詢費

(3) Spanish:
"No estoy facultado para ejercer la profesión de abogado y no puedo brindar asesoría legal sobre inmigración o ningún otro asunto legal como tampoco puedo cobrar honorarios por la asesoría legal."

(4) Korean:
저는 법을 집행할 수 있는 자격이 있는 변호사가 아니며, 이민이나 또는 다른 적법한 문제나 혹은 적법한 조언에 대한 수수료를 받을 수 있는지에 대한 법률상의 조언을 드릴수 가 없을지도 모릅니다.

(5) Haitian Creole:
MWEN PA AVOKA KI GEN LISANS POU PRATIKE LWA E
MWEN PA KA BAY KONSÈY LEGAL SOU ZAFÈ IMIGRASYON
OSWA NENPÒT KI LÒT ZAFÈ LEGAL OSWA AKSEPTE LAJEN
POU BAY KONSÈY LEGAL.

33

DEFINITIONS AND GENERAL TERMS

Acknowledgment

A formal declaration before a duly authorized officer by a person who has executed an instrument that such execution is his act and deed.

Technically, an "acknowledgment" is the declaration of a person described in and who has executed a written instrument, that he executed the same. As commonly used, the term means the certificate of an officer, duly empowered to take an acknowledgment or proof of the conveyance of real property, that **on a specified date "before me came ...., to me known to be the individual described in and who executed the foregoing instrument and acknowledged that he executed the same."** The purposes of the law respecting acknowledgments are not only to promote the security of land titles and to prevent frauds in conveyancing, but to furnish proof of the due execution of conveyances (*Armstrong v. Combs*, 15 App. Div. 246) so as to permit the document to be given in evidence, without further proof of its execution, and make it a recordable instrument.

The Real Property Law prescribes:

"**§303. Requisites of acknowledgments.** An acknowledgment must not be taken by any officer unless he knows or has satisfactory evidence, that the person making it is the person described in and who executed such instrument."

The thing to be known is the identity of the person making the acknowledgment with the person described in the instrument and the person who executed the same. This knowledge must be possessed by the notary (*Gross v. Rowley*, 147 App. Div. 529), and a notary must not take an acknowledgment unless the notary knows or has proof that the person making it is the person described in and who executed the instrument (*People v. Kempner*, 49 App. Div. 121). It is not essential that the person who executed the instrument sign his name in the presence of the notary.

34

Taking acknowledgments over the telephone is illegal and a notary public is guilty of a misdemeanor in so acting. **In the certificate of acknowledgment, a notary public declares: "On this .... day of .... 20 ...., before me came .... to me known,"** etc. Unless the person purporting to have made the acknowledgment actually and personally appeared before the notary on the day specified, the notary's certificate that he so came is palpably false and fraudulent. (*Matter of Brooklyn Bar Assoc.*, 225 App. Div. 680.)

Interest as a disqualification. A notary public should not take an acknowledgment to a legal instrument to which the notary is a party in interest. (*Armstrong v. Combs*, 15 App. Div. 246.)

Fraudulent certificates of acknowledgment. A notary public who knowingly makes a false certificate that a deed or other written instrument was acknowledged by a party thereto is guilty of forgery in the second degree, which is punishable by imprisonment for a term of not exceeding 7 years (Penal Law, §§170.10 and 70.00[2(d)]. The essence of the crime is false certification, intention to defraud. (*People v. Abeel*, 182 NY 415.) While the absence of guilty knowledge or criminal intent would absolve the notary from criminal liability, the conveyance, of which the false certification is an essential part, is a forgery and, therefore, invalid. (*Caccioppoli v. Lemmo*, 152 App. Div. 650.)

Damages recoverable from notary for false certificate. Action for damages sustained where notary certified that mortgagor had appeared and acknowledged a mortgage. (*Kainz v. Goldsmith*, 231 App. Div. 171.)

Administrator

A person appointed by the court to manage the estate of a deceased person who left no will.

Affiant

The person who makes and subscribes his signature to an affidavit.

Affidavit

An affidavit is a signed statement, duly sworn to, by the maker thereof, before a notary public or other officer authorized to administer oaths. The venue, or county wherein the affidavit was sworn to should be accurately stated. But it is of far more importance that the affiant, the person making the affidavit, should have personally appeared before the notary and have made oath to the statements contained in the affidavit as required by law. Under the Penal Law (§210.00) the wilful making of a false affidavit is perjury, but to sustain an indictment therefor, there must have been, in some form, in the presence of an officer authorized to administer an oath, an unequivocal and present act by which the affiant consciously took upon himself the obligation of an oath; his silent delivery of a signed affidavit to the notary for his certificate, is not enough. (*People v. O'Reilly*, 86 NY 154; *People ex rel. Greene v. Swasey*, 122 Misc. 388; *People v. Levitas* (1963) 40 Misc. 2d 331.) A notary public will be removed from office for preparing and taking the oath of an affiant to a statement that the notary knew to be false. (*Matter of Senft*, August 8, 1929; *Matter of Trotta*, February 20, 1930; *Matter of Kibbe*, December 24, 1931.)

The distinction between the taking of an acknowledgment and an affidavit must be clearly understood. In the case of an acknowledgment, the notary public certifies as to the identity and execution of a document; the affidavit involves the administration of an oath to the affiant. There are certain acknowledgment forms which are a combination of an acknowledgment and affidavit. It is incumbent on the notary public to scrutinize each document presented to him and to ascertain the exact nature of the notary's duty with relation thereto. An affidavit differs from a deposition in that an affidavit is an ex parte statement. (*See definition of* **Deposition**.)

Affirmation

A solemn declaration made by persons who conscientiously decline taking an oath; it is equivalent to an oath and is just as binding; if a person has religious or conscientious scruples against taking an oath, the notary public should have the person affirm. **The following is a form of affirmation: "Do you solemnly, sincerely, and truly, declare and** affirm that the statements made by you are true and correct."

Apostile

Department of State authentication attached to a notarized and county-certified document for possible international use.

Attest

To witness the execution of a written instrument, at the request of the person who makes it, and subscribe the same as a witness.

Attestation Clause

That clause (e.g., at the end of a will) wherein the witnesses certify that the instrument has been executed before them, and the manner of the execution of the same.

Authentication (Notarial)

A certificate subjoined by a county clerk to any certificate of proof or acknowledgment or oath signed by a notary; this county clerk's certificate authenticates or verifies the authority of the notary public to act as such. (See §133, Executive Law.)

Bill of Sale

A written instrument given to pass title of personal property from vendor to vendee.

Certified Copy

A copy of a public record signed and certified as a true copy by the public official having custody of the original. A notary public has no authority to issue certified copies. Notaries must not certify to the authenticity of legal documents and other papers required to be filed with foreign consular officers. Within this prohibition are certificates of the following type:

United States of America)
State of New York) ss.:
County of New York)
"I ...., a notary public of the State of New York, in and for the county of ...., duly commissioned, qualified and sworn according to the laws of the State of New York, do hereby certify and declare that I verily believe the annexed instrument executed by .... and sworn to before ...., a notary public of the State of ...., to be genuine in every respect, and that full faith and credit are and ought to be given thereto.

"In testimony whereof I have hereunto set my hand and seal at the City of ...., this .... day of ...., 20 ....

(Seal) (Notarial Signature.)"

Chattel

Personal property, such as household goods or fixtures.

Chattel Paper

A writing or writings which evidence both an obligation to pay money and a security interest in a lease or specific goods. The agreement which creates or provides for the security interest is known as a security agreement.

Codicil

An instrument made subsequent to a will and modifying it in some respects.

Consideration

Anything of value given to induce entering into a contract; it may be money, personal services, or even love and affection.

Contempt of Court

Behavior disrespectful of the authority of a court which disrupts the execution of court orders.

Contract

An agreement between competent parties to do or not to do certain things for a legal consideration, whereby each party acquires a right to what the other possesses.

Conveyance (Deed)

Every instrument, in writing, except a will, by which any estate or interest in real property is created, transferred, assigned or surrendered.

County Clerk's Certificate

See *"Authentication (Notarial)."*

Deponent

One who makes oath to a written statement. Technically, a person subscribing a deposition but used interchangeably with "Affiant."

Deposition

The testimony of a witness taken out of court or other hearing proceeding, under oath or by affirmation, before a notary public or other person, officer or commissioner before whom such testimony is authorized by law to be taken, which is intended to be used at the trial or hearing.

Duress

Unlawful constraint exercised upon a person whereby he is forced to do some act against his will.

Escrow

The placing of an instrument in the hands of a person as a depository who on the happening of a designated event, is to deliver the instrument to a third person. This agreement, once established, should be unalterable.

Executor

One named in a will to carry out the provisions of the will.

Ex Parte (From One Side Only)

A hearing or examination in the presence of, or on papers filed by, one party and in the absence of the other.

Felony

A crime punishable by death or imprisonment in a state prison.

Guardian

A person in charge of a minor's person or property.

Judgment

Decree of a court declaring that one individual is indebted to another and fixing the amount of such indebtedness.

Jurat

A jurat is that part of an affidavit where the officer (notary public) certifies that it was sworn to before him. It is not the affidavit.

The following is the form of jurat generally employed:

"Sworn to before me this .... day of ...., 20 ......"

Those words placed directly after the signature in the affidavit stating that the facts therein contained were sworn to or affirmed before the officer (notary public) together with his official signature and such other data as required by § 137 of the Executive Law.

Laches

The delay or negligence in asserting one's legal rights.

Lease

A contract whereby, for a consideration, usually termed rent, one who is entitled to the possession of real property transfers such right to another for life, for a term of years or at will.

Lien

A legal right or claim upon a specific property which attaches to the property until a debt is satisfied.

Litigation

The act of carrying on a lawsuit.

Misdemeanor

Any crime other than a felony.

Mortgage On Real Property

An instrument in writing, duly executed and delivered that creates a lien upon real estate as security for the payment of a specified debt, which is usually in the form of a bond.

Notary Public

A public officer who executes acknowledgments of deeds or writings in order to render them available as evidence of the facts therein contained; administers oaths and affirmation as to the truth of statements contained in papers or documents requiring the administration of an oath. The notary's general authority is defined in §135 of the Executive Law; the notary has certain other powers which can be found in the various provisions of law set forth earlier in this publication.

Oath

A verbal pledge given by the person taking it that his statements are made under an immediate sense of this responsibility to God, who will punish the affiant if the statements are false.

Notaries public must administer oaths and affirmations in manner and form as prescribed by the Civil Practice Law and Rules, namely:

- **§2309(b) Form.** An oath or affirmation shall be administered in a form calculated to awaken the conscience and impress the mind of the person taking it in accordance with his religious or ethical beliefs.

- An oath must be administered as required by law. The person taking the oath must personally appear before the notary; an oath cannot be administered over the telephone (*Matter of Napolis*, 169 App. Div. 469), and the oath must be administered in the form required by the statute (*Bookman v. City of New York*, 200 NY 53, 56).

- When an oath is administered the person taking the oath must express assent to the oath repeated by the notary by the words "I do" or some other words of like meaning.

- For an oath or affirmation to be valid, whatever form is adopted, it is necessary that: first, the person swearing or affirming must personally be in the presence of the notary public; secondly, that the person unequivocally swears or affirms that what he states is true; thirdly, that he swears or affirms as of that time; and, lastly, that the person conscientiously takes upon himself the obligation of an oath.

- A notary public does not fulfill his duty by merely asking a person whether the signature on a purported affidavit is his. An oath must be administered.

- A corporation or a partnership cannot take an oath; an oath must be taken by an individual.

- A notary public cannot administer an oath to himself.

- The privileges and rights of a notary public are personal and cannot be delegated to anyone.

Plaintiff

A person who starts a suit or brings an action against another.

Power of Attorney

A written statement by an individual giving another person the power to act for him.

Proof

The formal declaration made by a subscribing witness to the execution of an instrument setting forth his place of residence, that he knew the person described in and who executed the instrument and that he saw such person execute such instrument.

Protest

A formal statement in writing by a notary public, under seal, that a certain bill of exchange or promissory note was on a certain day presented for payment, or acceptance, and that such payment or acceptance was refused.

Seal

The laws of the State of New York do not require the use of seals by notaries public. If a seal is used, it should sufficiently identify the notary public, his authority and jurisdiction. It is the opinion of the Department of State that the only inscription required is the name of the notary and the words "Notary Public for the State of New York."

Signature of Notary Public

A notary public must sign the name under which he was appointed and no other. In addition to his signature and venue, the notary public shall print, typewrite or stamp beneath his signature in black ink, his name, the words "Notary Public State of New York," the name of the county in which he is qualified, and the date upon which his commission expires (§137, Executive Law).

When a notary marries during the term of office for which he/she was appointed, he/she may continue to use the name under which he/she was commissioned as a notary public. However, if he/she elects to use his/her marriage name, then for the balance of his/her term as a notary public he/she must continue to use the name under which he/she is commissioned in his/her signature and seal when acting in his/her notarial capacity, adding after his/her signature his/her married name, in parentheses. When renewing his/her commission as a notary public, he/she may apply under his/her married name or the name under which he/she was formerly commissioned. He/she must then perform all his/her notarial functions under the name selected.

A member of a religious order, known therein by a name other than his secular cognomen, may be appointed and may officiate as a notary public under the name by which he is known in religious circles. (Op. Atty. Gen., Mar. 20, 1930.)

Statute

A law established by an act of the Legislature.

Statute of Frauds

State law which provides that certain contracts must be in writing or partially complied with, in order to be enforceable at law.

Statute of Limitations

A law that limits the time within which a criminal prosecution or a civil action must be started.

Subordination Clause

A clause which permits the placing of a mortgage at a later date which takes priority over an existing mortgage.

Sunday

A notary public may administer an oath or take an affidavit or acknowledgment on Sunday. However, a deposition cannot be taken on Sunday in a civil proceeding.

Swear

This term includes every mode authorized by law for administering an oath.

Taking an Acknowledgment

The act of the person named in an instrument telling the notary public

SCHEDULE OF FEES

Appointment as Notary Public
   Total Commission Fee **$60.00**
   ($40 appointment and $20 filing of Oath of Office)

Change of Name/Address **10.00**

Duplicate Identification Card **10.00**

Issuance of Certificate of Official Character **1.00**

Filing Certificate of Official Character **1.00**

Authentication Certificate **3.00**

Protest of Note, Commercial Paper, etc. **.75**

Each additional Notice of Protest (limit 5) each **.10**

Oath or Affirmation **2.00**

Acknowledgment (each person) **2.00**

Proof of Execution (each person) **2.00**

Swearing Witness **2.00**

Made in the USA
Las Vegas, NV
09 August 2021

27861495R00028